I Took a Walk INTO THE WOODS

Energy medicine for your spirit and soul

STELLA GREEN

ISBN 978-0-9937118-2-4

stellatellsastory.com

About the Author

Stella Green grew up on the Lower North Shore of Quebec, in the small fishing village of Mutton Bay. With no television or any other electronic devices, Stella spent her days outside, fishing, exploring caves or digging for arrowheads left by her ancestors hundreds of years ago, or spending hours on the ocean, looking at the world beneath her father's boat.

Her connection with the land and sea has kept her spirit strong and free. And now, through her pictures and words, she hopes to inspire and give strength and freedom to your spirit as well.

I took a walk into the woods,
the forest floor beneath my feet.
Letting myself stay awhile,
into the mysteries of the deep.

I took a walk into the woods,
how far I went I do not know.
When I returned from the deepest part,
knowledge then began to flow.

I took a walk into the woods,
golden sun shone down on me.
Through all the leaves and branches wide,
love and peace and harmony.

I took a walk into the woods,
sweet flora filled the air.
And when I breathed so deeply,
it drew the ancients near.

I took a walk into the woods,
bare feet upon the ground.
And there I danced with the fairy folk,
twirling round and round.

I took a walk into the woods,
an eagle following from up high.
Together down a secret path.
Wisdom now, from earth and sky.

I took a walk into the woods,
an ancient rock became my friend.
Sharing things from long ago,
and how they will return again.

I took a walk into the woods,
no one else had ever seen.
Discovering ancient secrets,
the wisdom of the trees.

I took a walk into the woods.
I met an ancient pine.
And when I leaned against him,
his wisdom shared with mine.

I took a walk into the woods,
and there I felt at home.
And so I stayed for many days,
surrounded by companions, all alone.

I took a walk into the woods,
a whispering breeze close by my side.
Gently now, as it kissed my face,
I felt my soul open wide.

I took a walk into the woods,
and let myself be free.
to shed the layers of illusion,
remembering now, as it used to be.

www.ingramcontent.com/pod-product-compliance
Lightning Source LLC
Chambersburg PA
CBHW041526070426
42452CB00035B/21